FSC

www.fsc.org

MIX

Papier aus ver-
antwortungsvollen
Quellen
Paper from
responsible sources

FSC® C105338

Hans Bodmer

CDC

CONTROL DATA

The happy years with a spectacular
IT 'Phenomena': The Control Data
Corporation.

This book is an essay to bring some light to the
history of the CDC. Written by an 'insider' who
worked for the Company from 1964 to 1981.

This book derived from the announced interest from readers of the authors' recently published books 'The OTHER Computer History' and 'Die ANDEREN Computer Geschichten'.
It is an essay to describe and analyze the 'stormy' years of the CDC from 1957-2005.
The author's thesis and conclusion will lead to controversial discussions.

The services from Google, Wikipedia, and PONS were much appreciated. The help from Grammarly was pertinent.

I like to thank Werner Knecht for his contribution. The information obtained from the Facebook Control Data Corporation Private Group was helpful.

Please note that English is not the author's native language. He is fully aware that the applied writing style is 'personal'. And so are his handling of sentences, forms, and punctuation marks: Very liberal.

This here is Version 4 of the same title.

Production and publishing: BoD - Books on Demand, Norderstedt, Germany
ISBN: 9783746032795

Photo Back cover: Photo of the Author (In the presentation film from 1965 for the CDC6600 at CERN
https://videos.cern.ch/record/43172)

Index.

Prologue.

It is not so long ago…

The history of the development of IT could fill books with several hundred pages. A lot has happened in the computer world from John Neumann to Bill Gates. This book describes the short, but 'quirky' history of the American computer company Control Data Corporation, CDC. From 1957 to 2005. CDC was not even known to experts at first. In the old days, everything that had to do with computers was mostly commented on: "Ah, with those IBM machines." IBM and CDC were always in a highly fierce feud in the battle for market shares. IBM still exists.
Here is an incomplete list of disappeared IT giants: Remington, Sperry Rand, UNIVAC, Burroughs, Honeywell, DEC, PR1ME, and many more.
CDC had a relatively short, but all the more exciting and intense lifecycle. The author was like not many others heavily involved as an 'insider' from 1963 to 1981. During a conversation with his son Stephan, who has a degree in computer science, the author was urged to write down his experiences from the 'storm and stress years' of information technology.

Today, in the year 2023, computers are present everywhere. It is a daily tool used by humanity. And not only in the rich half of the world. But how many of the 'users' are aware of how we got here? And how many of the over eight billion human beings had ever heard of the CDC? Of course, CDC is not the only and undoubtedly not the most important of the failing companies.

But one of the most 'bizarre' ones.

1. Photo taken at CDC Headquarters 1966-07-01.

L to R: Gene B. Heywood, Walter G. Andrews, Frank C. Mullaney, Robert F. Leach, Seymour R. Cray, William R. Keye, William C. Norris, Chairman, with a model of the 6600 computer system.

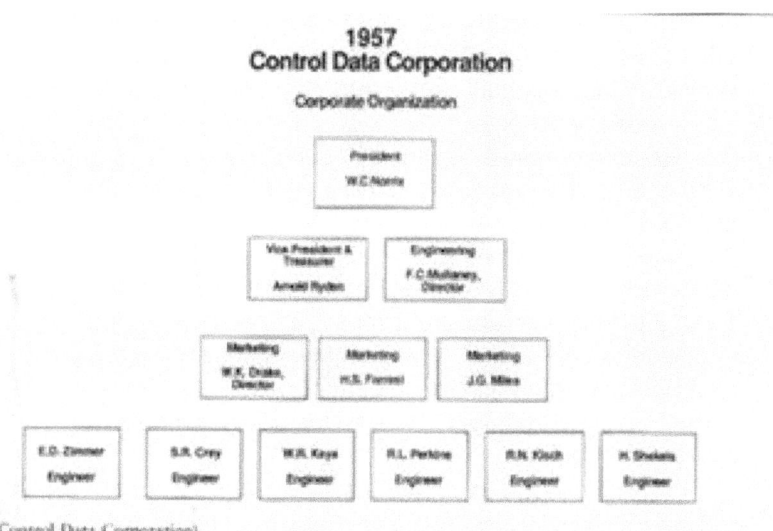

2. First CDC Organigram

7

2. CDC 1604 and CDC 160-A.

At the beginning of the revolutionary start of CDC were the first-generation transistor Computers CDC 1604 and CDC 160-A. Both were designed by one of the company's founders: The genius Seymour Cray. These machines succeeded greatly in universities, highest-level technical institutions, and leading future-oriented enterprises.

Called 'the father of supercomputing', Cray has been credited with creating the supercomputer industry.
Joel S. Birnbaum, the chief of technology of Hewlett Packard, said of him: "It seems impossible to exaggerate the effect he had on the industry. Many things that high-performance computers now do routinely were at the farthest edge of credibility when Seymour envisioned them."

In 1950, Cray joined Engineering Research Associates (ERA) in Saint Paul, Minnesota, a former United States Navy laboratory that had built code-breaking machines, a tradition ERA carried on when such work was available. ERA was introduced to computer technology during one such effort, but at other times had worked on a wide variety of basic engineering as well.
Cray was quickly regarded as an expert on digital computer technology, especially following his design work on the ERA 1103, the first commercially successful scientific computer. He remained at ERA when it was bought by Remington Rand and then Sperry Corporation in the early 1950s. At the newly formed Sperry Rand, ERA became the scientific computing arm of their UNIVAC.

Cray, along with William Norris, another founder of CDC, later became dissatisfied with ERA, then spun off as Sperry Rand.

In 1957, they founded a new company, the famous Control Data Corporation.

By 1960 they had completed the design of the CDC 1604, an improved low-cost ERA 1130 that had an impressive performance for its price. Even as the CDC 1604 was starting to ship to customers in 1960, Cray had already moved on to designing other computers. He first worked on designing an upgraded version, the CDC 3000 series. But company management wanted these machines targeted toward business and commercial data processing for average customers. Cray did not enjoy working on such 'mundane' machines, constrained to design for low-cost construction so that CDC could sell many of them. He desired to produce the fastest computer in the world.

After some basic design work on the CDC 3000 series, he turned that over to others and worked on the CDC 6600. Nonetheless, several special features of the 6600 first started to appear in the 3000 series.

The name 1604 was not at all popular amongst the marketing managers. Nobody but Cray alone knew for a long time where the name came from. It derived from the ERA model 1103 Seymour worked on and the Address of CDC's first computer manufacturing plant, 501 Park Avenue, Minneapolis.

The 160-A was designed by Cray during three days of treatment at a hospital. That's was the author heard. Or was this just another of those rumors surrounding Cray?

It had 4096 12-bit words of core memory and an instruction set of 64 instructions. Those were mostly designed to control the peripheral devices.

Later, the 6000 series PPUs used the same instructions.

The ETH (Eidgenöschische Technische Hochschule = Federal Polytechnic School in Zürich) bought the first CDC 1604 in Europe. Before they built ERMETH, one of the first Computers in Europe.

9

3. CDC 1604

4. CDC 160-A

5. ETH Zurich, Switzerland

6. ERMETH, built at ETH.

3. CDC 3000 Series Computers.

The upper 3000 series used a 48-bit word size. The first 3000 machines to be produced was the CDC 3600. They were first delivered in June 1963. The CDC 3400 and CDC 3800 were shipped in December 1965. These machines were designed for scientific computing applications. They were the upgrade path for users of the CDC 1604 machines. However, these machines were overshadowed by the upcoming 60-bit CDC 6000 series machines when the CDC 6600 was introduced in 1963 and delivered in 1965. Some high-end computer Labs purchased 3000 series machines as stopgaps while waiting to deliver the ordered 6600 machines. CDC had indicated that the 6000 machines would use the same assembler language. The lower 3000 series used a 24-bit word size. They were based on the earlier CDC 924, a 24-bit version of the CDC 1604. The first lower 3000 to be released was the CDC 3200 (May 1964), followed by the smaller CDC 3100 (February 1965) and the CDC 3300 (December 1965). The final machine in the series, the CDC 3500, was released in 1967 and used integrated circuits instead of discrete components. The 3300 and 3500 had optional relocation capabilities floating-point arithmetic and BDP (Business + Data Processing) instructions. These machines were targeted toward business and commercial computing.
As such, they were not directly competing with the later 6000 machines.

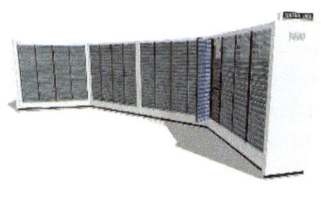

7. CDC 3600　　　　　8. CDC 3000 Series Mainframes

4. The 6000 series machines.

As said, the 6600 was THE success of the CDC. It was the so-called 'Flagship'.

It was followed by the CDC 6500, a dual CPU machine. Then came the 6400 with a single CPU and mostly used as a frontend machine for the 6600. Then there were the 6200 and the 6700. Neither of them was very successful.

The CDC 6000 series computers were an astonishing success in the 70is. And they brought the money.

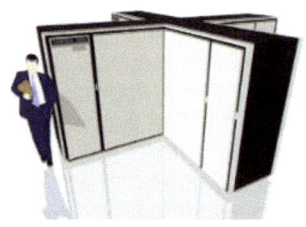 

9. CDC 6600 as seen by an Artist   **10. CDC 6600 in Reality**

11. CDC Mainframes

12. 6600 from another Angle

13. 6000 Series Console

14. 6000 Series Transistor Module

15. 6000 Series Memories

5. The famous CDC 6603 Disk Drive.

The first 6600 were delivered with the very expensive CDC 6603 Discs. Seymour Cray once told the author: "This is our best piece." This is, of course, not at all true. The 6600 mainframe was by far the best IT equipment ever built. This is, at least, the opinion of the author.

The 6603 was not built by CDC itself. It was the successor of the Bryant Model 2. They were made by the Bryant company in Detroit by German toolmakers. As the CE (Customer Engineer) trainees were many times proudly told by the instructor.

It was a very impressive gear. The magnetic discs themselves had a diameter of about 150 cm. The read/write heads were positioned by a hydraulic system using pressured oil.

The heads had to be positioned with an exactitude of a micrometer within fractions of a millisecond.
The capacity was rather limited: Approximately 37 Mega 6-bit bytes.

A curiosity: The LRL (Livermore Radiation Lab) demanded that the disk be burnt when the device was taken out of service. So that no information once written on them can get to the Russians…

These disks were very popular with the CE's and the operating personnel. They were used as tabletops for garden tables. Those became therefore very popular.

16. Bryant Model 2

17. CDC 6603

18. CDC 6603 (open doors)

6. CDC Tape Stations.

The 606 and 626 Magnetic Tape Stations were not built by CDC either. CDC bought the magnetic tape division from Bendix. Bendix was, at the time, a leading electronic equipment company.

CDC took over its magnetic tape drives division and specialized engineers.

 CDC supplied its employees with tie clips and the females with arm bracelets. Those had stones of different colors and qualities. The first gift was given at the start of the employment and had a green stone. The next one after 5 years of loyalty with a stone of a different color. The from Bendix taken-over people got the stones for the years they worked for Bendix. This was not at all appreciated by the CDC staff.

The CDC 626 was a flop. By far not the only one.
It used magnetic tape the size of an inch. Normal tapes were ½ inch wide.
One of the problems was that the role of the tape was heavy. The second was this: It was very difficult to correctly align the 14 bits in a row.

19. CDC Bracelet   **20. CDC Tie Clip**

21. Magnetic Tape   **22. Messed up Magnetic Tape**

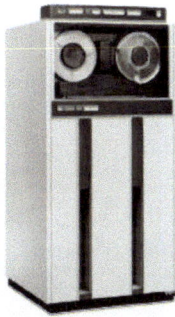

23. Old Magnetic Tape Station   **24. CDC 606 Tape Station**

25. Tape Stations in Action   **26. Magnetic Tape Storage Hall**

7. Drum Storage and Portable Disc Packs.

The next higher level of storage units was the drum. Again, they were huge and expensive machines. With a relatively rather limited capacity, but with a very fast access time. With a mean time between failure rate which was even worse than the 6600 Mainframe in their first phase in production.
CDC themselves did not build drum storage devices.
The next generation of mechanical storage devices, the disk-pack drive, was much more reliable.
In size like kitchen chairs. But don't ever sit on it! Then on the cover is a knob to open the drive and to mount and exchange the portable disc-packs.

A very practical unit. Every programmer and system analyst could store and carry away his own data. Only the data needed by the in CPU executing programs had to be online.

Something also worth to be mentioned is the following: The disc-packs were only a few grams lighter as was allowed by the government to be carried by female personnel.

27. First Generation Drum   **28. Newer Drum**

18

29. Portable Disc Pack

30. Early Disc Pack

31. Disc Pack Drive

32. Disc Pack Driver Array

8. CDC's Employment 'Methods'.

For the author began at the end of 1963 a new life.

At first, he had no idea what would come at him.
His experiences with the 'matter' seemed to be what he was learning in the first grade of primary school. So to speak: In the ancient world of computer science. Or, at least, it seemed that until then, only the early Middle Ages were reached.
He was tired of the daily, almost tedious work. He had no fun anymore with the machines from BULL. The work with them became monotonous. There were fewer and fewer of those famous and needed challenges. And as it looked, a Gamma 3 cannot be sold in Switzerland. Let alone in Zurich. And he was still relatively young. Even when he often appeared to be old. Primarily when his troubleshooting was not accomplished in the desired time.
Something new had to be found. And with BULL, there was nothing in sight. It was only when the company later merged with Honeywell and became Honeywell-Bull that drastic changes were coming. But Honeywell brought in the 'pepper', the modern computers. The mechanical equipment which handled the punched cards was brought in by BULL and then incorporated into the joint venture.
He had not to through the merger. He left BULL before. He was not genuinely thankful to the company, which, at least, enabled him to start his professional career. And also paid for it.

Immense happiness suddenly happened.

The opportunity which so surprisingly arrived was too irresistible not to be taken. What 'wonder' was this?
The Control Data Corporation, the CDC.
The job advertisement in the newspaper by this American company, which was utterly unknown to him and almost all non-specialists, stated something like this: We are looking for technicians for our supercomputer CDC 6600 just sold to CERN (Center European de Recherche Nucléaire) in Geneva.

Computer experience, good English skills, and the willingness to get trained in the USA and then work in Meyrin GE were the requirements they asked for.

By the way, the entire 'deal' had brought CDC, as he heard much later, over eight million, in 1964 in the reasonably hard Swiss Francs.

He hardly believes that he could get such an attractive job. Lack of relevant experience with transistor computers. But who had them back then? And with his rudimentary English learned in evening courses in a private language school.

Quote: "He who risks nothing wins nothing."

He immediately called the Zurich office of CDC Switzerland. A gentleman who spoke Swiss German was on the phone and introduced himself: "I am the chief secretary and also for the time the director of CDC Switzerland." As it turned out later, the Swiss subsidiary consisted only of the boss, three secretaries, two programmers, and a technician.

The gentleman invited him for an interview. It will take place in the next upcoming two days. The engineer from Minneapolis, responsible for the hiring, will only be here for a short time. They apparently were under terrible pressure. Courses started in Minnesota in March. It was already late November!

For such an opportunity, he will drop all other of his activities. So, he immediately accepted the day and the time of the interview.

The gentleman was pleased: "Good. And send us the usual recruitment needed document via express mail to the Zurich address. I will translate them into English. The manager from Minneapolis doesn't speak a word of German."

Speaking German is not to be expected from a Midwestern American. But first, he had to search on a map where Minneapolis and Minnesota are located. It is west of the Mississippi. The state borders its northern side to Canada.

Then the interview took place. He was quite a bit more than just nervous when waiting in the reception room in the chic office in an expensive building near the Paradeplatz in Zurich.

There were computer magazines in English on a tiny glass table in the waiting room. He loosely leafed through them. He understood almost nothing. But he learned that this machine, the CDC 6600, was admired and praised everywhere. As the most modern, the leading, and the most powerful of what has been brought onto the market so far. Sounds already very promising! But is he the man for it?

Will see!

He had to wait endless long minutes. Another candidate was at the interview.
Meanwhile, the secretary chatted with him in a friendly manner and did not even ask specific questions. The door opened. The other applicant said: "Goodbye." In accent-free Oxford English. A plump, jovial medieval gentleman now greeted him in the broadest 'Yankee slang'. The man was not dressed in a suit like him. But in jeans, sneakers, and a gray T-shirt. The Chief engineer sat opposite him at an elegant meeting table. The 'Ami' started slowly to talk to him.
The interviewer looked at him quite incomprehensibly. He had probably asked a question and was waiting for an answer. He, the job applicant, answered from now on. Less with words, but with gestures of affirmation or negation. Depending on the expressions that flit across the face of the man who vividly reminded him of a cowboy.
After half an hour, he was relieved from the painful 'procedure'. He wanted now to shake hands with the engineer. The man stared at him with astonishment. Apparently, shaking hands is not so common in the Midwest.
The secretary seemed to have impatiently waited for the end of the interview because he immediately came to him and asked: "How did it go? Are you employed?" He lied: "It went..." Now he was very, very embarrassed. This was visible to his counterpart. He whispered, extremely ashamed: "You must ask the gentleman from Minneapolis." The secretary then did so. Also, in Swiss German-colored English and certainly not in the US jargon. To his great astonishment, the 'cowboy' nodded. And mumbled something like: "Mister Fischer is responsible for contract details such as wage, training, and so

on." Then the apparently hungry man went to the door with a sturdy step and asked: "Where's the nearest MacDonald?"

The unexpected finale came now. The secretary said: "You got the job! Employment begins on March 1st. We will discuss everything else later."
Everything else didn't matter to him now. It will be fine for sure. But what came now had to come! Mr. Fischer said, yes, he almost shouted: "But now English has to be learned with full concentration!!!" That was a stringent Swiss military command tone.

Now the first action was to cancel his work contract with BULL. He didn't even think that leaving BULL could cause serious difficulties. The employment contract contained a clause that specifies that the employee is not allowed to work for a competitor for three years after the dismissal. This clause he would, if needed, encounter: "CDC is not a competitor. They are technically too far ahead."
This was the beginning of a very significant time for him.
The education to become a CE, Customer Engineer, began only a few weeks later in Minneapolis and Chippewa Falls.

The education was by far not completed there. Back in Geneva, he had to attend several special courses, mainly at CDC's European training center in Frankfurt, Germany. In the first year, the schooling rooms were rented in a chubby center of the town.
It was located in the middle of the 'red light' district of the city. When he left the building after a hard night shift, he was often approached by one of the 'belles for a night'.

33. Training Center in Frankfurt, Germany

9. Minneapolis, Minnesota. ('Minnehopeless')

Why Hopeless?

That was the word the director of the Hospital Universaire de Geneve informatics department used when talking about Minneapolis. This showed the director's frustration when the man was dealing with the CDC's software crew working on the promised TOOS (Transaction Oriented Operating System). One of the reasons the hospital bought a CDC 6000 machine was exactly this OS that had never seen the light of the real world. So, the hospital programmers build their version, namely DIOGENE.
The author, at that time a senior analyst with several years of experience in operating system programming, was 'condemned' to work at the hospital. This was because CDC did not fulfill the contractual agreements. TOOS was just another of the CDC's software flops.

The author's first days in the US are worth to be mentioned. On March 13th, 1964, Swissair flight number 100 from Zurich to New York had him on board. After arriving, he had to struggle through US entry control. With more than just a critical eye from the controlling officer. But his business visa classified 'B4' apparently calmed the guy. Then he passed through customs control. His only suitcase was not even opened but immediately thrown to the grim-looking black-muscled baggage porter behind the entrance control.
The trip continued with Northwest Orient Airline.
The airplane was half empty. Therefore, the extremely friendly, smiling flight attendants. They were dressed in the airline's colors: Blue-yellow and still wearing skirts. A can of Coca-Cola and a reasonably eatable sandwich were for free. Of course, only in a cardboard cup and without a plate. He did not care. He was already dead tired. He almost missed the approach to the airfield of the 'Twin City' Minneapolis-St. Paul Airport.

He was shaken briskly by the roar of the winter storm outside. The landing made him more than only slightly trembling. The pilot needed three approaches to get the airplane onto the ground.

With still fragile legs, he was picked up by a fat, always laughing, jovial gentleman and immediately driven to a hotel in the city's center. The man said something like that he was responsible for the trainees from Europe. And then he added: "I will guide you to the training center on Monday". At least that's what he thought to have understood. Or better, that is what he guessed. Good night! There will be a significant problem in learning this rudimentary American English, that they were speaking here.

Monday was the first day of school. The first part of the theoretical training, which lasted three weeks, started.

The female instructor's welcome speech was relatively 'cool' and without a handshake. The other trainees were all Americans from different states. He heard this from the lively discussions they had before the beginning of the class. He realized this, despite his more than only basic and very incomplete English.

For the following weeks, language was his biggest problem. In the more prestigious private language schools, such as the one he went through, one learns to ask: "Where can I park my Rolls-Royce?" But not how to order a hamburger in Minneapolis.

At first, there was no mention of hardware. They had first to learn to program. Already the next day, they were obliged to write a small program. In the programming language FORTRAN (Formula Translation). FORTRAN was one of the first higher-level programming languages. Of course: Invented by IBM.

There was no computer in the hotel, but a card-puncher. The punched cards were then sent to the computing center in the headquarters, and the results were delivered the next day.

His first program consisting of ten FORTRAN statements resulted in ten FORTRAN errors! A bitter disappointment! He was so firmly convinced that he had understood and implemented everything correctly.

After three weeks, as announced, the practical training began. This now occurred in the factory in Bloomington, a western suburb of Minneapolis. The company's headquarter was also located there. The suburb is about 10 miles, more than 16 kilometers, away from the city center.

To commute between downtown and Bloomington, a car will be provided for him. No question about a valid driver's license. Of course, it was assumed that he had such a one. In Switzerland, he was 'only' allowed to drive a motorcycle, and he had permission to learn to drive a car. He only had a few hours of driving practice with the shaky Volkswagen of his apprenticeship colleague.

He kept the fact of not having a driver's license for himself. He wanted to avoid being 'shipped' back to Zurich immediately.

The car was ready for him next Friday evening. The car key was handed to him without any questions.

Most of the cars had left the vast parking area. So, he found 'his' car immediately, an older Ford. Luckily, not a Cadillac with a gigantic tail. The modest Ford was therefore much easier to manipulate. It was now time for him to drive around a few rounds in the vast, empty parking lot. Then he activated all the possible courage and 'trembled' home. In the now very little traffic and luckily broad, wide streets. A long search for a large parking lot followed.

Intensive personal driving school on Saturday and Sunday was needed. And it worked without too much-unwanted strangling of the motor.

On Monday morning, he had to get up very, very early. To be in Bloomington before the usual morning traffic jam.

The next stage of the training was then in Arden Hills. This is an Eastern suburb of Minneapolis on the other side of the 'old man river'.

The construction of the building was, at that time, not even finished. An immense flat structure with no windows. The interior was straightforward. The partitions between the small offices are made of plywood. In the middle was the room for meals. Equipped with vending machines and automates, which spat out boiling black stuff. The training room was a bit larger. With stools without a backrest. They were not so necessary because most of the discussions were done standing up. And those were loud, intensive, and very frequent. It was gesticulated wildly with arms and hands.

There were more than only a few uncertainties about what they were told by the very insecure teacher. So, the telephone to the Lab in Chippewa Falls in western Wisconsin was running hot. There, the machine was developed.

But there is no question about its most modern architecture and hardware. The 6600 was three times faster than the previous record-holder, the IBM 7030 Stretch. This alarmed IBM. At that time CEO, Thomas Watson Jr. wrote a memo to his employees: "Last week, Control Data announced the 6600 system. I understand that in the laboratory developing the system, there are only 34 people, including the janitor. Of these, 14 are engineers, and 4 are programmers. Contrasting this modest effort with our vast development activities, I fail to understand why we have lost our industry leadership position by letting someone else offer the world's most powerful computer". Cray's reply was sarcastic: "It seems like Mr. Watson has answered his own question."

Another of Seymour's quotes was this: "It is not enough to build the fastest CPU. More important is the performance of the overall system."

Now, a different story from downtown Minneapolis.

He now rented a small and poorly furnished 'studio' in a shabby brick building located just at the border of a slum. The building contained only one-room apartments. But very cheap.

On the same level lived a little young lady next door to his. Like in the so beautiful and praised song and popular pop hit 'Living next door to Alice'. Is it not also her first name?

She spoke very little. The first time they talked to each other was in the hotel 'Normandy Village'. This was a popular meeting place for the city's singles on Saturday evenings. With a piano bar. There you sit, female and male, around a large concert piano. The pianist plays popular folk songs. Those who can sing or have drunk enough sing-along. The 'Budweiser' beer, which was very expensive for him, did not really taste good. But it cost a whopping 80 cents and had to be paid immediately in cash. Compare this to the fact that a gallon of petrol at that time cost a lousy 18 cents!

The beer was usually consumed standing up. The places to sit around the piano were reserved for regular guests. So, not for him.

And he was soon also already a bit 'messed' up.

Until he saw something, which immediately woke him up: The lady from next door!

Very nicely dressed, white blouse, black skirt, fishnet stockings, and high-heels.

It almost took his breath away.

Her steps fluctuated slightly. But she recognized him. She answered his greetings in more than just broken English. And, of course, she immediately asked: "Where are you from?". Her second question was, as usual, at the beginning of a flirt: "What are you doing here?" He replied: "I work with computers." In a kind of admiring look at him and getting somewhat gently blushing. She says predicatively:

"Ah, with these IBM machines?"

34. Park Avenue 501   **35. McGill Building Entrance**

36. Bloomington Headquarters   **37. Headquarter later.**

38. Arden Hills Facility, still under construction

10. Chippewa Falls, Wisconsin.

The chance to get to know Seymour Cray personally became concrete. Because now he was transferred to Chippewa Falls. In the factory, or better, the laboratory, where the 6600 was built. At the time, the 'monster' was still in development. It will take years until the supercomputer worked more or less error-free. In particular, the software.

The laboratory is located next to Cray's birth house and idyllically situated on the banks of a picturesque little river. An environment that will soon, autumn be approaching, becoming more and increasingly colorful.
Seymour and his crew were about to finish the machine with serial number 3. The one that was ordered by CERN. It must be delivered in January next year (1965). The engineer who was, among others, then responsible for it, namely him, can therefore deal with the pitfalls of serial three from the very beginning. And there were more than enough of those.

The operator console of the 6000 series machines was also the most modern of the modern. Until now, the control units were long, flat boxes like large tables. They were equipped with push buttons or mechanical switches and little lamps. LEDs (Light-Emitting Diodes) were at that time far from being available.
The numbers and letters appear on the front of the two cathode-ray tubes. They are 'chased' there by a voltage of 15,000 volts. This device was always admired by everybody and not only by him. From further away, the display tubes look like the enormous eyes of prehistoric frogs. Does the name 6600 come from those? The two zeros could have been derived from the two eyes of an animal.
Seymour Cray has subordinated himself to the Marketing Manager and no longer named the new machine with one of his own fantastical associations.

The author's first practical action was adjusting the wire length between the modules. Why 'tune' the wire length? Can't one just use the shortest possible wire?

Not at all! Because there are short-term registers with a length of 120 bits. For example, for buffering double-precision floating-point numbers. Twenty modules were needed for this. They all are timed by the same clock pulse. That's why the length of the wire between the clock pulse distributor and the modules must be the same. This necessity thickened the 'mattress' of the cables behind the chassis enormously. The control was carried out by observing the incoming pulses using a cathode ray oscilloscope, which simultaneously records four different signals.

Soon, a big problem occurred. Misunderstandings came up for everyone, including Seymour. The perfidious difficulty was only found after weeks.

The switching time of the chosen transistors must, according to the specifications, be between four and five nanoseconds. Now, there were two separate deliveries of those. The first had a switching time of just below the upper tolerance limit. The second delivery had a switching time just above the lower guideline. But all were within the specified time. So, where was the problem? In retrospect, simple: If 20 transistors with the longer switching time were connected in series, then the total time for a signal to pass was 18 nanoseconds longer than the time when 20 transistors with the faster switching time were connected in series. This discrepancy was deadly for the proper functionality of certain instructions dealing with double-precision numbers.

The mood, the team spirit, and the mutual respect of all employees engaged in the Lab, almost only of the male gender, were excellent. Very, very rarely a loud word or even a heated discussion. Only once did he see Seymour angry. A marketing manager from the headquarters wanted him to write a COBOL (Commercial and Business Oriented

31

Language) compiler. Seymour knows precisely that the 6600 was not built for business applications. The 'marketing freak' was promptly thrown out of the Lab by Seymour. But once, the genius was also very satisfied. Another of his creations was sold. For roughly 2 million dollars. He ordered to buy all real French champagne to be found in Chippewa Falls. There were only three bottles available!

To his excitement, the 'father of Supercomputers' took his time to chat with a Swiss 'learner', namely him, in front of the Lab in the most beautiful sunny weather. They sat quietly in the front of the building, drinking a cup of coffee together. Once, Seymour organized a meeting of foreign trainees with the members of the local Rotary Club, where Seymour was an active member. There were three trainees from Europe: A colleague from Germany, he, and a specialist for cooling devices from Geneva. This man was absolutely needed for the maintenance of the 6600.
They were invited for dinner in the only hotel in town and afterward interviewed by the editor of the local newspaper. They appeared in the paper the next day on the front page. With a group photo entitled: CDC educates engineers from Europe.

.

39. Chippewa Lab

40. Outside the Lab in Winter

41. Downtown Chippewa

42. Leinenkugel's Brewery

43. 6600 Wiring

44. 400000 Transistors!!!

11. CDC at CERN.

The CDC 6000 Series computers are powered with 60 and 400 Hertz AC. However, the voltage, which is common in Europe, has a frequency of 50 Hertz and must therefore be converted.

Why 400 Hertz? Quite simply because the conversion to direct current is easier to achieve. The conversion to DC is performed in the 6000 series machines themselves.

Four huge converters were installed in a kind of machine hall specially built for this purpose. Why two each? Not because of their performance. But, because of the highly unlikely case of a failure of one of the converters. In the computer world, at least one or more technical resources as the reserve are a must. The whole room looks like the generator hall of a small hydropower plant. Huge electric motors are mechanically coupled with equally huge generators. Those machines create a loud noise of around 90 decibels. It is so big that it could still be heard in summer through the then-open doors in the nearby 'Village' Meyrin, 5 kilometers away. And accordingly, also provoked the expected complaints by the people living there!

Most of the maintenance engineers lived there too. This 'fact' was a good one. Because in the case of the frightening and, unfortunately, too frequent breakdowns of the system, the man on duty could immediately request help from others. The team functioned exceptionally well. It could happen that everyone was at the same time at the same party. One phone call was enough and the entire CDC staff in Geneva, including managers, salesmen, and software specialists, were in the computer room at nearly 'lightning' speed'.

Not only in the event of a breakdown were 'all men on deck'. A tremendous exercise soon came at them. All wires between the chassis in one cabinet to the other had to be replaced in a 'night and fog' action (a German expression for something that must be done at night and should not be seen by anybody). This was done over the weekend. About 2000 cables had to be replaced. The reason for this was discovered very late: The small adapter plugs required to connect the cabinets had not been tinned carefully enough. As a result, the material eroded and fractions of a nanosecond of the impulses flowing through the wires got lost. They had to be replaced by connectors coated with a nanometer-thick cover of gold. Only two connections of over 2000 were incorrectly wired. A masterpiece by all those involved.

At CERN, there was a little fidgety and always nervous Dutchman. A genius in what numbers is concerned. Among other things, the man could quote the SBB's (Swiss federal trains) timetable by heart. He told him once: "The 6600 is great. When it works!"
And then there was the computer 'witch'. A petite, not-so-good-looking Englishwoman. A very, very talented and brilliant programmer. She could get outraged, and then she shouted so loud that the screams even exceeded the noise of the generators. And then, like a witch, she rushed away. Without a broom, but with a massive stack of paper under her arm and cursing loudly.
And then there was the typical Scottish gentleman, a Mac... A doctor of mathematics and the head of computer science at CERN at that time. He was not at all angry about the current unreliability of his risky acquisition. He must have known that a Supercomputer like the 6600 has its 'birth pains'.
After all, the 6600 at CERN set the at that time the world record for calculating the famous number 'Pi' with 50 thousand digits after the comma.

There is a unique real story worth mentioning because it occurred in the author's career only once: The total fallout of one of the two large display tubes of the control console! This problem was not the case for him. Because he was not a radio nor TV electrician. And unfortunately, he could not learn FEAM.

The very high tension needed for the console tubes terrified him also terribly. Fortunately, he had a good colleague, a certified electrical engineer. The man first had great fun proving his capability to fix the momentary only 'one-eyed' console.
Not for a long time!
The specialist soon found out that a condenser in there has burned out. The problem was therefore clearly recognized immediately and can thus be solved in a relatively short time. But this time, it was not repaired as fast as desired. Because in the local CDC spare parts warehouse, there were no such components. And this part could not be found throughout the entire CERN.

Quote: "Necessity is the mother of invention.

His colleague reacted very fast. He raced home in his old VW Beetle. There he took his TV apart. He found there the so much-needed capacitor with precisely the right capacity!

The situation was saved once more...

Another problem was the vulnerability of the core memory units. Those were very expensive. One unit cost, at that time, as much as a new beetle VW, nearly 8000 CHF. Their repair was not easy. The crew at CERN suspected that the spare units they received were not even repaired. So, they marked the units to be sent to be fixed with a tiny hand-marked 'C', standing for CERN, under the top metal cover plate. All new incoming allegedly repaired units were checked immediately. If such a 'C' was there, then they were placed at the end of the local queue of spare units or even sent back right away without even first trying to use it.

CERN had a costly maintenance contract that required a technician to be present 24 hours. The agreement also covered holidays, like Christmas and New Year's Day. No problem for him. He was not necessarily a friend of festive days. Especially in hours without technical problems, on weekends, and during holidays, something at that time was very new and also very popular. And it killed the sitting around and waiting to be helpful.

What was this? The Baseball Game at the operation control console. It was probably the first game ever programmed for a 'von Neumann' machine.

Indeed, very cleverly programmed by someone who unfortunately remained unknown to him.

A little stick figure appears at the bottom of one of the console's display tubes. Above was another. The most crucial man in real baseball: The pitcher. At the push of a key, the virtual pitcher 'throws' the baseball down toward the virtual batter. Sometimes fast, sometimes slow, sometimes straight, sometimes in a curve. Just like in American baseball. The batter at the bottom of the console must now react. The player at the console had to press one of the two programmed keys on the keyboard. Depending on the speed of his reaction and the intensity of the keystroke, the 'baseball', a small dot on the screen, fly away or sneaks slowly along the bottom line.

In the best case, this results in a 'home run'. This is the best result that can happen in real baseball. If not, then, depending on the batter's reaction, there are points given or nothing at all. The results are displayed on one of the screens.

45. CERN, Main Entrance   **46. CDC Crew at CERN**

12. The first approach to Computer Networks.

The author was there when computer networks were emerging. He had chanced the job and is now an Operating System programmer working in CDC's software development Center in Sunnyvale, California. The CDC software was, for the most part, 'caused' in the 'Silicon Valley' between San Francisco and San Jose. With a climate far more humane and more moderate than the one in Minnesota.

He needed a while to moderate his typical 'Teutonic' stubbornness, stop his profile neurosis, and adapt to the mentality of the Californians.

His usual demands for a certain office comfort had to be profoundly reduced. Because his office was located in a more or less temporarily constructed building. But it was prepared for earthquakes. It was situated a little outside the village. In a not very overbuilt area. Surrounded by vast fields planted with tomatoes and the like.

The building was almost identical to the one in Arden Hills. Quadratic, one floor high, with thin wooden walls, provisionally painted in light gray. Windows were only available on the first floor. This was the floor of the 'chiefs'. Depending on their position in the hierarchy, they had an office with an outside view. The windows could not be opened. In the four corners of the building were the offices of the best-paid executives.

The rest of the 'workforce' had offices inside the building. In the so-called 'six-packs'. This name was derived from the until today used packaging of six small Coca-Cola bottles. The six offices were separated by thin walls that formed a unit. They had all the same size, 2x4 meters. Each was occupied by two 'slaves', the 'normal' programmers, as he was one of them. The telephone calls made or received by the 12 occupants in a six-pack could be heard by everyone. Also, the very personal, intimate gossip if it was not whispered.

It was also loud in the 'jail'. The offices had to be cooled. The air conditioning of the building was also cheaply built. That's why the noise level was, to say the least, very high. The card-puncher machines to write the programs were situated in the corridors and were very much in demand. To get hold of one, he had to reserve it at least one day before. Time on the computer to test the programs was even scarcer. So, at three in the morning, there was sometimes a gap for using the computer alone.

And he had to be alone! Because his code would bring the machine into a software crash was more common than not. He soon adapted to the given situation and took over the practices of his 'buddies'. For example, to place the required lists, punched cards, and magnetic tapes on an office chair with rolling wheels and then push everything into the computer room when it was finally free for one hour.

The first task of the beginner from Switzerland, namely him, was to enable the use of the expensive disk space by more than just one computer. So only one copy of the data can serve several machines. And, what is more important, several mainframes can over this medium 'talk' to each other.

The coordination of the traffic between the connected machines was a colossal challenge. Especially the locking of the access. It must never be possible for the disc-accessing processes of the connected computers to get in each other's way.

First, this entirely new approach was called the 'multi-mainframe' feature. It was the first step in one of the greatest inventions in the IT world:

The Computer Networks!

Not many inventions on earth had a similar impact on humans.

The Network Communication System concept and the products discussed now were a significant change in

Control Data's priorities in developing future products. This future is now oriented toward the world of data communications and networks. With the CDC CYBER 170, the Network Operating System (NOS), and the Network Communication System (NCS), the task of information movement takes its place as a co-equal with the job of data processing. To the CDC salespeople, this meant the necessity to understand better the data communications environment and the new CDC products. To the CDC CYBER system user, it means having the ability to plan and implement effective computer networks.

Computer Network Structure's primary objective is to use a computer system to its maximum. This can be accomplished in various ways. In recent years, technical advances and cost reductions in both computers and communications facilities have created a strong trend toward the accomplishment of this objective by providing access to computer power through the use of communications networks. As a result, an ever-increasing number of companies are buying data processing services or developing their own computer networks to take advantage of scale and resource sharing. The relaxation of tariff restrictions and increased competition will cause further expansion of digital networks, microwave systems, and satellite communications facilities. This aspect of higher quality, lower-cost communications will accelerate this trend toward computer networks.

The upcoming networks needed unique hard and software equipment for the task of controlling and handling the local and global telecommunication requirements. The existing mainframes and even the superminis could not handle this.

47. SVLOPS

48. Sunnyvale Village

13. The first step toward the interactive use of computers.

After Sunnyvale, he was back at CERN. And it began another whole new and fundamental chapter in the history of IT. The development in the direction of making it possible for a user to have direct access to the big mainframes had started.
The application programmer can 'speak' directly with the machine. He does not need to punch his very long programs on cards and have them read in by an operator. And then have to join the long queue of those waiting for the results.
He can now type his program into the main memory. A huge step forward in the still early, but very important, phase in the history of computer science!
He was very amazed when he could use it for the first time. Until now, such a possibility was only a highly desirable 'Utopic'.
The first input devices were simple mechanical telex machines. They were soon replaced by the so-called monitors. Those were, today one would say, 'primitive' TV sets. Of course, still without a microprocessor or other 'intelligent' electronics. A monochrome TV with a keyboard. Nothing more and nothing less.

In CDC's COS, the program to control the interactive use of the computer was the so-called 'Editor'. It was written in FORTRAN. This program was a 'product' produced by one of his close friends.

This 'Editor' was probably one of the first in the category of re-entrant programs. This means that a single system program can at the same time simultaneously process the programs of several users.

Software is known as a product like tropical fruits. It rips at the customer side.

The Editor was also far from being 'ripe' when the first provisional version was delivered to CERN. But this new possibility for everyone to become, as the author puts it in German: Mit dem Computer per 'DU', was sensational!

Also for the TH Berlin. A very well-known technical university. They bought a CDC machine. With very kind support from the German government in Bonn and the Berlin Senate.
It was long before the fall of the wall.
The clever leaders of the university immediately recognized the potential of the upcoming trend of interactive computing.
His friend and creator of the multi-user editor were ordered to Berlin. He was also sent there to become familiar with the program.
The Editor program had one crash 'landing' after the other. His friend and creator could experience and correct his 'bugs' on the spot.
The schooling took place in a large lecture room. With more than a dozen monitors. And very interested and greedy students. And a multi-user program that did not survive 15 minutes. The famous mean time between failures was at a record-breaking minimum.
It was clear that he did not give the Berliner the fact that he also works for CDC. Why? He was ashamed of what his friend had created.

The time of interactive computing was started and with it, the need for local and later global networks.
A completely new type of hardware device is entering the game.
The first generation of devices to do this were simple, already existing minicomputers.

The CDC 2550, Cyber17, Cyber 18, and Cyber 1000 were the minicomputer used by the mainframes as the front end. Their task was to control the now upcoming interactive use of the mainframes by the users.

Also later, the whole complex steering of the data networks was done in those minis.
They can be considered the predecessor of today in use routers. They were 16-bit minicomputers that were primarily used in real-time environments.

2550 was a product of CDC's Communications Systems Division in Santa Ana, California (STAOPS). STAOPS also produced another communication processor (CP), used in networks hosted by IBM mainframes. This M1000 CP, later renamed C1000, came from an acquisition of Marshall MDM Communications. A 3-board set was added to the Cyber 18 to create 2550. The Cyber 18 was generally programmed in PASCAL, Assembler, FORTRAN, BASIC, and RPG II. Operating systems included RTOS (Real-Time Operating System), MSOS 5 (Mass Storage Operating System), and TIMESHARE 3 (time-sharing system).

Cyber 18 was just a new name for System 17, based on the 1784 processor. M1000/C1000, later renamed Cyber 1000, was used as a message store and forward system by the Federal Reserve System. A version of the Cyber 1000 with its hard drive removed was employed by Bell Telephone. This was a RISC processor (Reduced Instruction Set Computer). An improved version known as the Cyber 1000-2 with the Line Termination Sub-System added 256 Zilog Z80 microprocessors. The Bell Operating Companies purchased large numbers of these systems in the early 80tis for data communications.

First, there were the LANs (Local area networks), and the WANs (Wide Area Networks). The WLAN (Wireless Local Area Networks) was at that time an absolutely utopic dream.

The upcoming age of networks, local and global, could not be managed and handled by the traditional mainframes, and the minis like the CDC 2550 or even the superminis like the PDP11 were soon at their limits.
The market badly needed an entirely new type of equipment.

They were not built by IBM, and surely not by CDC.
The first and until today the leading company to build routers was CISCO. The name CISCO is derived from San Francisco. The golden gate bridge was for a long time the company's emblem.
CISCO Systems was founded in December 1984 by Leonard Bosack and Sandy Lerner, two Stanford University computer scientists who had been instrumental in connecting computers at Stanford. They pioneered the concept of a LAN being used to connect distant computers over a multiprotocol router system. By the time the company went public in 1990, CISCO had a market capitalization of $224 million, by the end of the dot-com bubble in the year 2000, this had increased to $500 billion, surpassing Microsoft as the world's most valuable company. As of December 2021, CISCO had a market capitalization of around $267 billion.

A small fraction of it would have kept CDC alive, but Bill Norris invested in education and social engagement.

LAN Network Architecture.

49. Star, Classic

50. Ring, IBM Token-Ring

51. BUS, Ethernet

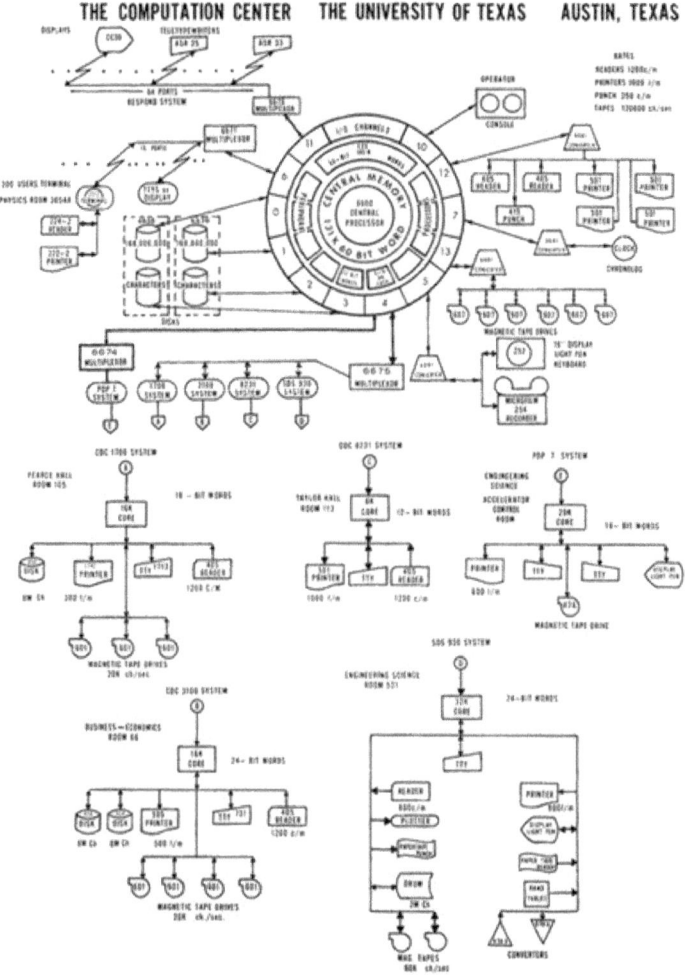

52. Example of a Private Network

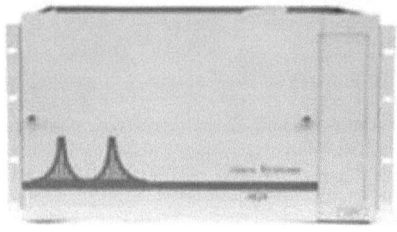

53. CISCO AGS Router

14. The 'chaotic' Cyber Series Story.

The Cyber line included five different series of computers.

The Cyber 70 and Cyber 170.
They were based on the architecture of the CDC 6600 and CDC 7600 supercomputers, respectively.
The Cyber 70 and 170 architectures were successors to the earlier CDC 6600 and CDC 7600 series and therefore shared almost all of the earlier architecture's characteristics. The Cyber-70 series is a minor upgrade from the earlier systems. The Cyber-73 was essentially the same hardware as the CDC 6400 with the addition of a Compare and Move Unit (CMU). The CMU instructions speeded up the comparison and moving of non-word-aligned 6-bit character data. The Cyber-73 could be configured with either one or two CPUs. The dual CPU version replaced the CDC 6500. As with the CDC 6200, CDC also offered a Cyber-72. The Cyber-72 had identical hardware to a Cyber-73 but added additional clock cycles to each instruction to slow it down. This allowed CDC to provide a lower-performance version at a lower price point without developing new hardware. It could also be delivered with dual CPUs. The Cyber 74 was an updated version of the CDC 6600. Cyber 76 was essentially renamed CDC 7600. Neither the Cyber-74 nor the Cyber-76 had CMU instructions. The Cyber-170 series represented CDCs' move from discrete electronic components and core memory to integrated circuits and semiconductors memory. The 172, 173, and 174 use integrated circuits and semiconductor memory, whereas the 175 uses high-speed discrete transistors.

The Cyber 180.
They were developed by a team in Canada, and released in the 1980s..
Cyber 180 development began in the Advanced Systems Laboratory, a joint CDC/NCR development venture in 1973 and was located in Escondido, California. The machine family was initially called Integrated Product Line (IPL) and was intended to be a virtual memory replacement for the NCR

6150 and CDC Cyber 70 product lines. The IPL system was also called the Cyber 80 in development documents. The Software Writer's Language (SWL), a high-level PASCAL-like language, was developed for the project with the intent that all languages and the operating system (IPLOS) would be written in SWL. SWL was later renamed PASCAL-X and eventually became Cybil. The joint venture was abandoned in 1976, with CDC continuing system development and renaming Cyber 80 as Cyber 180.

As the computing world standardized to an eight-bit byte size, CDC customers started pushing for Cyber machines to do the same. The result was a new series of systems that could operate in 60- and 64-bit modes. The 64-bit operating system was called NOS/VE and supported the virtual memory capabilities of the hardware. The older 60-bit operating systems, NOS and NOS/BE, could run in unique address space for compatibility with the older designs. The actual 180-mode machines are micro-coded processors that can support both instruction sets simultaneously. Their hardware differs entirely from the earlier 6000/70/170 engines. The small 170-mode exchange package was mapped into the much larger 180-mode exchange package. Within the 180-mode exchange package, there is a virtual machine identifier (VMID) that determines whether the 8/16/64-bit two's complement 180 instruction set or the 12/60-bit one's complement 170 instruction set was executed.

Cyber 200 series.
In 1974, CDC introduced the STAR architecture. The STAR is an entirely new 64-bit design with virtual memory and vector processing instructions added for high performance on a particular class of math tasks. The STAR's vector pipeline is a pipe that supports vector lengths of up to 65,536 elements. Unfortunately, the latencies of the vector pipeline are very long, so peak speed is approached only when very long vectors are used. The scalar processor was deliberately simplified to provide room for the vector processor and is relatively slow compared to the CDC 7600. As such, the original STAR proved to be a great disappointment when it

was released (see Amdahl's Law). Best estimates claim that three STAR-100 systems were delivered.

It appeared that all of the problems in the STAR were solvable. In the late 1970s, CDC addressed some of these issues with Cyber 203. The new name kept with its new branding, and perhaps to distance itself from the STAR's failure. The Cyber 203 contains redesigned scalar processing and loosely coupled I/O design but retains the STAR's vector pipeline. Best estimates claim that two Cyber 203s were delivered or upgraded from STAR-100s.

Cyberplus or Advanced Flexible Processor (AFP).
Each Cyberplus (Advanced Flexible Processor, AFP) is a 16-bit processor with optional 64-bit floating point capabilities and has 256 K or 512 K words of 64-bit memory. The AFP was the successor to the Flexible Processor (FP), whose design development started in 1972 under black-project circumstances, targeted at processing radar and photo image data. The FP control unit had a hardware network for conditional micro-instruction execution, with four mask registers and a condition-hold register.

At least 21 Cyberplus multiprocessor installations were operational in 1986. These parallel processing systems include from 1 to 256 Cyberplus processors providing 250 MFLOPS each, which are connected to an existing Cyber system via a direct memory interconnect architecture (MIA). This was available on NOS 2.2 for the Cyber 170/835, 845, 855, and 180/990 models.

That's more than enough from the CDC's Cyber machines.

Comments from the author: He feels sorry for those who have read this chapter. And he believes that IT specialists will agree with him: The Cyber Program was clearly much 'over-stressed'!
Wasn't it even a 'tohuwabohu'?

Questions: Wouldn't less be more?

54. CDC 2550/Cyber 18

55. CDC Cyber 180

56.CDC Cyber 170

57. CDC Cyber 205

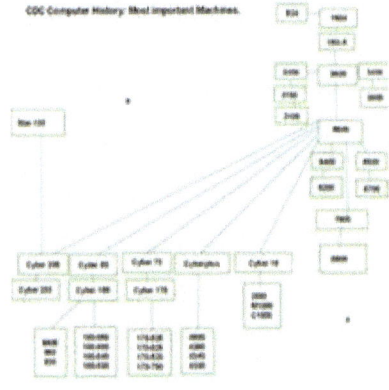

58. CDC Computer History

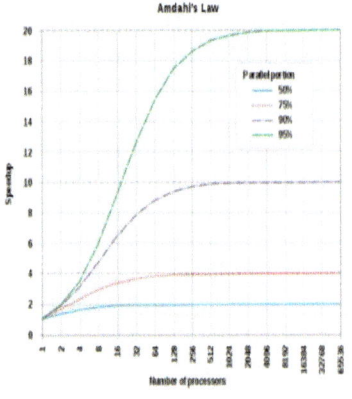

59. Amdahl's Law

Cyber Series Megaflops Rating.
(as found on the Net)

Megaflops		Software
32	CDC Cyber 2000V	F0RTRAN V2
17	CDC Cyber 205 4-pipe	FTN
17	CDC Cyber 205 2-pipe	FTN
12	CDC Cyber 990E	FTN V2 VL=HIGH
9.4	CDC 4680	f77 2.11.2 o2
5.1	CDC 4330-300 33 Mhz	f77 2.20 -03
4.8	CDC Cyber 875	FTN 5 OPT=3
4.6	CDC Cyber 176	FTN 5.1 OPT=2
4.0	CDC Cyber 4360	f77 2.11.2 o2
3.7	CDC 4320	f77 2.20 opt=02
3.5	CDC 4330	f77 2.20 opt=02
3.3	CDC 7600	FTN
3.1	CDC Cyber 960-31	NOS/VE 1.3.1 FTN 1.6
3.0	CDC Cyber 4340	f77 2.11.2 o2
2.6	CDC Cyber 760	FTN5 OPT=3
2.1	CDC Cyber 180-860	NOS/VE OPT=HIGH
2.1	CDC Cyber 175	FTN5 OPT=2
2.0	CDC 7600	Local
1.8	CDC Cyber 175	FTN5 OPT=1
1.6	CDC Cyber 180-850	NOS/VE OPT=HIGH
1.6	CDC Cyber 170-750	FTN 5.1 opt=3
1.2	CDC 7600	CHAT, No opt
0.99	CDC Cyber 180-840	NOS/VE OPT=HIGH
0.58	CDC Cyber 930-31	NOS/VE 1.2.2

15. Why this dispersion of resources?

CDC, was it only a supercomputer company?
Wrong!
CDC has a vast list of products they made themselves, or were heavily involved.

Control Data Institute and other subsidiaries were ok.

But what did the CDC have to do in the commercial credit business?

Commercial Credit Corporation (from Wikipedia):
In 1968, Commercial Credit Corporation was the target of a hostile takeover by Loews. Loews had acquired nearly 10% of CCC and intended to break up on acquisition. To avoid the takeover, CCC forged a deal with CDC lending them the money to purchase control of CCC instead, and that is how a computer company came to own a fleet of fishing boats in the Chesapeake Bay.

By the 1980s, Control Data entered an unstable period, which resulted in the company liquidating many of its assets. In 1986, Sandy Wells convinced the Control Data management to spin off their Commercial Credit subsidiary to prevent the company's potential liquidation. Over a period of years, Weill used Commercial Credit to build an empire that became Citigroup in 1999. Commercial Credit was renamed CitiFinancial. In 2011, the full-service network of US Financial branches was renamed OneMain Financial.

Service Bureau Corporation (from Wikipedia):
At one time, IBM announced a new System/360 model, the Model 92, which would be just as fast as CDC's 6600. Although this machine did not exist, sales of the 6600 dropped drastically while people waited for the release of the mythical

Model 92. Norris did not take this tactic, dubbed fear, uncertainty, and doubt (FUD), lying down. In an extensive antitrust lawsuit launched against IBM a year later, he eventually won a settlement valued at $80 million.
As part of the settlement, he picked up IBM's subsidiary, Service Bureau Corporation (SBC), which ran computer processing for other corporations on its own computers. SBC fits nicely into CDC's existing service bureau offerings.

For the last time the question: Wouldn't less be more?

It was Bill Norris's nature: To be involved and at the center of everything.

Attached are ads for, even for insiders like the author, very unknown CDC products.

Ask
CONTROL DATA
about their full range
of Engineering Services.*

They have them all.

- Installation and maintenance of CDC computer systems, worldwide
- Third party maintenance (non-CDC systems)
- Computer facilities site planning
- Design and construction management of computer centers
- Computer facility support services
- Worldwide parts & logistics support
- Refurbishment of both CDC and non-CDC equipment
- Radio and data communications maintenance
- Installation, test, and repair of medical electronic equipment
- Technical training for customers

*Control Data offers you a complete spectrum of maintenance agreement options and prompt, highly professional attention, tailored to your needs. Call CDC collect (612) 893-7800 for more information or write CDC, Box 1980, Twin Cities Airport, St. Paul, MN 55111

CONTROL DATA CORPORATION

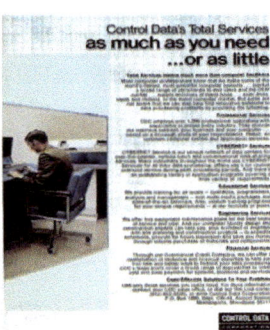

60. Engineering Services

61. Laser Beam

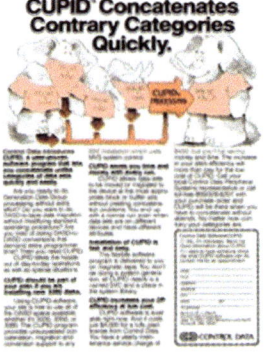

62. Cupid

63. Total Services

64. Omega 480

65. ???

66. Ask Control Data Drive

67. 516 Megabit Disc

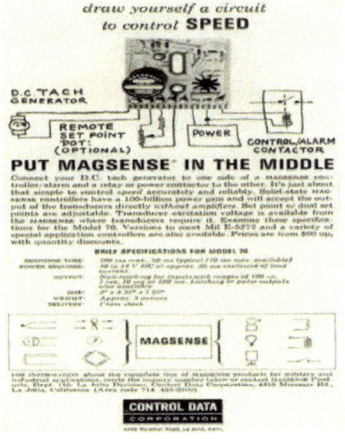
68. CEDAR?   **69. MAGNESE?**

Browse through our general store of computer products and services.

CDC' Cyber 70 Computers

Control Data® Cyber 70 is a family of computer systems. Medium-scale through large to super-scale. You can start with the smallest model. Grow to the most powerful system in the market today, if you need it. All without extensive, costly reprogramming. Economic benefits include high throughput per dollar and excellent price/performance ratios plus the ability to handle up to 15 full programs simultaneously. And CDC Cyber 70 Systems will work with up to 500 remote terminals.

M1000 Communication Systems

Our data communication system speeds information between terminals and your central computer. Messages are received, edited, routed, translated, delivered, intercepted or stored—completely within the system. With the M1000 handling communication and related administrative functions, your computers can concentrate on rapid processing of data. And M1000 is modular. So you can add to it as your data network grows.

OCR Systems

CDC has Optical Character Reading equipment to fill virtually any performance or budget requirement. From a totally new, low-cost laser scanning system that handles large-scale volumes demanding fast and accurate data conversion. To a proven page-reading system with economic throughput. To a versatile combination page and document reader which reads up to 90,000 documents an hour. We've even installed special, super-scale scanning systems to provide all necessary input for a data base of 50 million records.

Peripherals

Regardless of the make (or size) of your computer, chances are excellent that you can find the peripheral equipment you need "on the shelf" at Control Data. Some recent additions to our line include a new cartridge disk drive which provides 25 million bits of random storage, a 200-line-per-minute line printer and a 300-card-per-minute card reader. Check our capabilities before selecting your next peripheral devices.

Terminals

Control Data offers a complete line of graphic, batch and interactive terminals. From large terminals with a full set of peripherals to small desk-top CRT display stations. Plus many in between. We also provide terminal operations control systems to make your data network operate more efficiently. Our terminal product line is designed to provide peak performance. Flexibility. And economy. Whether you have a CDC computer, or another make.

Consulting Services

Sometimes you may need expert data processing assistance. To initiate a project, put one back on track, or evaluate results of a project you have completed. Control Data can help at any stage. Our professional consultants bring in a comprehensive understanding of particular business and industrial problems. With their broad experience in systems analysis, they can develop cost/benefit reports to simplify management decisions. We can also design and develop new applications software for you. Or modify available software to meet your specific needs.

70. General Store

16. The 'Triumphal March' of the Superminis and the PC.

In the late 70tis began the extinction of the supercomputer 'dinosaurs'. There were still some creations coming from Cray. And the Japanese also began to produce high-tech supercomputers. CERN and ETH bought an NEC.

But now the time of the 'Superminis' was coming. He had heard the complaints of his salesmen colleagues: "The superminis are breaking our necks. CDC has to make something which can compete with the newcomers like, for example, DEC (Digital Computer Corporation), PR1ME, Data General, and others." For example, PR1ME's computers came close to the giants' performance for a fraction of the price. Regarding data communication and computer networks, PR1ME was higher advanced than CDC. In the capability to connect machines from different manufacturers with one another, PR1ME was also superior to CDC.
The salesman responsible for a critical existing CDC customer, a leading machine manufacturer in Winterthur near Zurich, told him: "Have a look at what PR1ME can do!"

And they can really do a lot better than CDC! He was soon convinced of this.
With the up-coming of the superminis, CDC had no chance in the commercial, education, and smaller universities markets. The lower ends of the cyber 170 and 180 machines were highly overpriced for them. Thy maintenance and upgrade costs were by far just not affordable for non-government financed enterprises.
Upgrade a classic machine with more memory brought CDC and also IBM long night shifts. In the superminis, this was accomplished within hours.
Therefore, the quotation by the German-speaking mini-computer maintenance engineers: IBM stands for 'Immer bis Mitternacht' (always until midnight) or 'Ich bin müde' (I am tired).

The prices for upgrading the supermini with one megabyte of core memory were also moderate. A customer in Geneva, a high-quality steel wholesaler, told the author once in French: Ca goute deux fois rien (this costs two times nothing).

Another reason for the success of the superminis was that most of them delivered their systems with the popular UNIX (Uniplexed Information and Computing System) or similar proprietary ones.
These operating systems were more straightforward to use than the much more complex NOS versions from CDC.

Not only the upcoming superminis was a significant fact in recline of CDC revenues: The very accelerating use of the PCs did hurt the manufacturer of the classic mainframes. Most of them did not, so to say, 'jump on the wagon' and did not participate in the enormous new business challenge.
With one exception: IBM. And they did well!
CDC was considering that the personal computers were a passing fad: A significant management error!
Which was a big surprise to the author. Typically, Bill Norris took a chance to get involved in any available computer-oriented and not-so-computer-orient new product.
He was not the only one. Ken Olson, at that time CEO of DEC, was failing too. He never believed in a world with a computer on every office table.

71. Supermini PR1ME 300

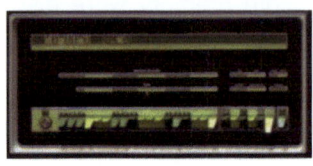

72. Supermini DEC PDP11

73. First IBM PC

74. CDC enters the PC Market

17. The UBISCO Debacle.

Another primary reason for that CDC 'vent down the hill' was the UBISCO (Union Bank Informatics System Concept) project!

Schweizerische Bankgesellschaft (SBG) and the Control Data Corporation started the UBISCO project in the early 1970s. It was the project's goal to automate all SBG's banking operations with the help of one colossal computer system. Unfortunately, four years after the project had been started it was given up.

What now follows is an attempt to uncover the reasons for this failure, and thus to explain to researchers and historians why so often extended computer projects are not successful.
Large European banks, and giant Swiss banks, differ dramatically from large US banks because of the Swiss legal environment and payment patterns. The legal environment in Switzerland has always allowed banks to operate in all financial sectors customer accounts, payments, credits, funds management, and securities trading. Consequently, most Swiss banks are universal banks active in all segments of the financial industry. In the past, Switzerland's payment patterns were largely cash-based. Checks never gained any significance in Switzerland, and salaries and wages were generally paid in cash until the 1960s when banks began introducing special accounts for salary payments. In addition, wholesale banking banks focused on serving large corporations and wealthy individuals. Services included commercial credits, stock exchange transactions, securities administration and management, and foreign exchange for international payments. In brief, Swiss banks processed a high volume of complicated financial transactions, which were not easily automated.
The Union Bank of Switzerland and Control Data Corporation started the UBISCO project in the early 1970s. The project should have automated all the bank's operations with a single CDC computer system, but UBISCO failed four years later. Unraveling the project's failure might help researchers and

historians learn why such large computer projects are so often unsuccessful.

The author was (today he says: fortunately) only a little involved in the gigantic 'illusion'.

The 'deal' was in the order of many millions of dollars. The existing software was far away from being ready to be used. CDC sold the bank a so-called 'paper tiger'. A term used in computer business jargon for something that only exists on paper. In the past, the 'enemy' IBM was often accused of doing this.
The CDC's Cyber series were highly unsuitable for commercial applications. Seymour Cray was fully aware of this. But not the 'clever' Swiss salesmen and the management of CDC Switzerland.
The project UBISCO, based on the promised TOOS (Transaction Oriented Operating System), was from the beginning doomed to fail. The giant technical effort, enormous costs, and never-ending complications resulted in a fiasco.

Created, most likely in hell. And In California and Zurich.

A new version of the 'cabbage' was flown to Switzerland weekly. Accompanied by one of the specialists. Or even by a more or less pretty secretary who also once wanted to visit Zurich.

There everybody was for a long time in a very much unmotivated euphoria. CDC Switzerland gave a huge party. All employees in Switzerland were invited. Even those in Geneva. Also, he and his family. So, about 120 employees. And everybody with partners, and when they had, children. It took place in a well-known castle in the center of Switzerland. The participants arrived in reserved SBB (Schweizerische Bundesbahn = Swiss national trains) first-class wagons. With champagne breakfast included. After arriving at the hotels, the children were taken care of immediately by hostesses and servants. The boys and girls were not seen anymore until the next day.

The celebration itself took place in the feudal old castle-like building. The guests were welcomed by fanfare blown by medieval costumed, professional wind instrument players. The dinner, of course, was the finest of the fine. Accompanied by Vivaldi, played by a small chamber orchestra. Then, of course, as usual at such events, endless speeches or better, also, as usual, self-praises. Loud applause after each of the 'palavers. For him, these speeches were rather dull and tiring.
Everybody was in a great mood. There was jubilation, joy, and cheerfulness. And all were enthusiastic and satisfied with what was offered.

Quote: "Arrogance comes before the fall."

And the fall came soon. The whole UBISCO project collapsed. Crashed into rubble and ashes! This was since a long time written in the sky. An end with horror. Just a little better than an endless horror.
The reason why?
In the humble opinion of the author: Most of the CDC machines were not built for commercial applications.
They don't have instructions that process single characters. Byte-oriented in/output was not possible. The proposed machines needed, for efficient interactive use of the CPU, specialized front-end computers. And the ones from CDC were far away from being capable of accomplishing the very demanding response-time requirement.

Quote: "Except for expenses, there was nothing."

And those expenses were enormous. According to first heard rumors, the author heard: Fifty million Swiss francs. For both CDC and the bank. He does not know if these figures include the logically following costs for lawyers and tribunals. To the detriment of technology historians, the bank still kept the files of the UBISCO project under key and lock until recently.

But today, the actual facts are open.
The first charge by UBS at a Zurich court was CHF 72'907'066.
CDC Countercharge was over CHF 103''000'000.

After heavy discussions, the final 'deal' was that CDC paid back 23 million CHF for tacking back the hardware, which cost the bank 40 million.

75. First UBS Headquarters　　　　　　　**76. UBS Emblem**

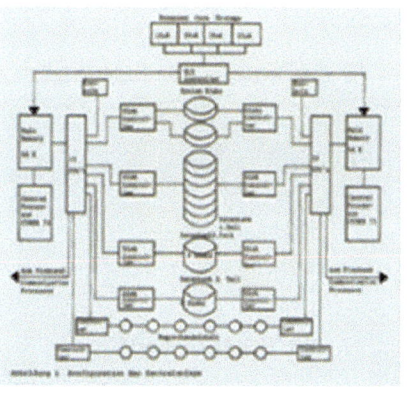

77. UBISCO Utopia

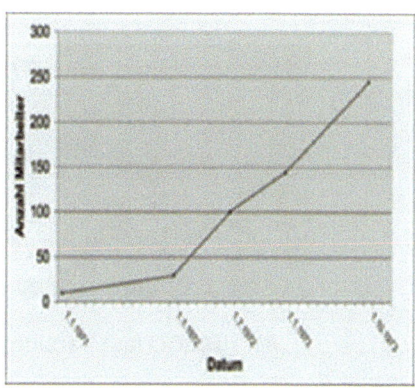

78. UBS People involved

79. TOOS (no comments…)

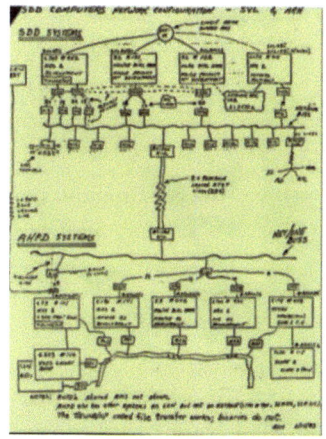

80. Handmade Software

81. UBISCO last Version   **82. UBISCO Mood**

83. Château Lenzburg, UBISCO Celebration

18. The 'Grounding' of a Giant.

UBISCO was most likely one of the biggest flops in the history of IT.
But more catastrophes followed soon.

For the author, the most severe happened at CERN. Here in Switzerland. They had bought a CDC 7600. The successor of the 6600. Even more compact, even denser modules. Now with small flat but still concrete transistors. 4x4 mm square-shaped and one millimeter thick. With switching times of less than one nanosecond. And there were over half a million of those.

He no longer had to repair the new machine. He was now a 'Supercomputer softy'.
But he had nothing to do with the software for the 7600. Good for him, because the existing operating system, SCOPE, did never run properly.

Another disaster, this time not a technical one, came soon. As said, such disasters do rarely come alone. Not much later, the already by that time UBISCO flop badly shocked Swiss branch of the once leading supercomputer company was hit again. CERN did not buy the second 7600. This was so long-waited and hoped for. And was financially terribly needed.

CERN bought an NEC (Nippon Electronic Corporation).

Quote from a Swedish colleague: "The 'shit' hit the ventilator." Sorry for the profane wording, but it was the right quote at the right time.

The once glorious company was moving downhill faster and faster. And steeper. Staggering flops like the OS of the beginners' SIPROS, PLATO (Programmed Logic for Automatic Teaching Operations), a futuristic project of an electronic schooling system pampered by the founder and CEO of CDC

William C. Norris, and other management failures shoveled her grave. In addition, the catastrophic flop of the 'most super' of all supercomputers: The STAR-100 and the cyber 200 series machines. Only a few saw the real light of the world.

Question: Did the complex and confusing Cyber Program bring any profit?

Seymour Cray left the sinking ship. While working on the CDC 8600. Which never reached the market under this name. But now was started the advent of something very interesting and new under the sun: The CRAY RESEARCH in Denver, Colorado.

The author is sure about this: After Cray left CDC, the 'exit' was accelerated. Nobody could replace the Genius.

CERN 'forgot' CDC. Only a minimal number of service personnel was still needed. The author was completely superfluous.

In the 1980s, CDC was left primarily as a hard disk manufacturer, and their series of SCSI drives were particularly successful. But at this point, the rest of the company crashed, and the board started pressuring Norris to step down. They were particularly harsh in blaming his social programs for their problems, although any connection is difficult, if not impossible, to find.
Norris eventually realized there was little he could do to stop this course of action, and started an effort to place the company under the leadership of two hand-picked replacements. The stockholders didn't agree, and Norris subsequently retired in January 1986. His successor as Control Data CEO was Robert M. Price.

Price began his professional career for CDC as a mathematician staff specialist. His responsibilities there expanded to software sales and services, international sales, and several executive positions, culminating with serving as president and the chief executive officer from 1986 to 1989.

The final end.

As the demand for high-performance mainframes fell, CDC had various financial problems and what remained of the company was finally purchased by Syntegra 1999, a data-mining firm.

The following article was found on the net:

Los Angeles Times
By JAMES FLANIGAN
April 19, 1989

Money talked on Monday when Control Data withdrew from the competition in supercomputers. It couldn't continue financing a money-losing but technologically advanced operation, said its Chairman, Robert Price.

The pullout is a bad sign, but not for the reasons you may think. It's not that the United States, the country that worries about its schools turning out enough engineers, is falling behind in technology. In fact, there is little doubt that the U.S. industry leads in supercomputer technology.

It was U.S. financial markets that failed Control Data. The real story is that the nation that turns out more business school graduates than any other is threatened competitively because it cannot figure out how to finance a business over the long pull, and how to stay the course when the going gets rough.

Supercomputers, machines that can perform billions of mathematical calculations per second, are important. They are used today to design airplane wings, simulate weapons systems, find oil deposits, and decipher photographs from outer space. In the next decade, as their powers increase, so will their value and importance.

Yet sadly, Control Data, the Minneapolis company that first developed such computers in the early 1970s, threw in the towel even though it turned out that they built one of the world's most powerful supercomputers. Its ETA Systems computer had technical flaws and needed software. But Control Data has sold 34 ETAs worldwide within the global market which has seen only 409 supercomputers sold to date.

And with time, Control Data might have rejiggered its machine and developed the software. But nobody would take a chance on it. Banks wouldn't extend their credit lines, and the stock market seemed happy to accept its decision to close the business and restructure. The speculators said the company was not increasing shareholder value. And this is the only 'thing' which counts in the business world...

Control Data's departure leaves the U.S. industry with two prominent supercomputer players: Cray Research as the global leader, with more than 200 machines sold. And the giant IBM, which had declared its intention to enter the field with the backing of the entrepreneur Steve Chen's company Supercomputer Systems Inc. A variety of supercomputer start-ups round out the U.S. industry.

U.S. Strengths.
What are the U.S. strengths? Technical brilliance and venture entrepreneurs, who are advancing the state of the art. Both Cray Research and Supercomputer Systems were going beyond big single-processing machines to parallel-processing ones. Those break down massive problems, get many parts of answers quickly, and put them back together, as you might do in developing a satellite photograph.

The U.S. industry also is bringing new power to supercomputing with an effort by Intel Corp., the semiconductor company, to put together 2,000 chips, with 1 million transistors each, to produce the most powerful computers yet made. Intel is working under a contract from the Defense Department on that advanced development.

But most U.S. financing is entrepreneurial. Cray Research, now grown to $800 million in revenue, was founded by Seymour Cray, 62, who left Control Data in 1972 to form his own firm with backing from Control Data. Two years ago, Steve Chen left Cray to form Supercomputer Systems and attracted backing from IBM.

This is exciting, but the staying power of small firms is suspect. Gary Smaby, a supercomputer specialist for Needham & Co., an investment bank that backs start-up companies, believes the next decade will demand larger firms with the resources for a high-stakes game. Control Data, after all, lost $100 million in supercomputers in one year.

Without patient financing, home-grown technology may leave home. Two promising newcomers in supercomputers are already owned or backed by Japanese companies: Key Computer Labs, of Fremont, Calif., was recently bought by Amdahl Corp., of which Fujitsu owns 45%, and Solbourne Computer of Longmont, Colo., is backed by Matsushita.

"Capital is a competitive threat," says Intel's President Andrew Grove, who sees Japanese financing being offered to start-up companies up and down Silicon Valley. But does it matter who finances technology? Yes, says Grove: "because control of technology leads to jobs and development for your people and leadership for your country."

True enough, but unless U.S. financial markets recognize there are values other than shareholder values, that leadership will fade.

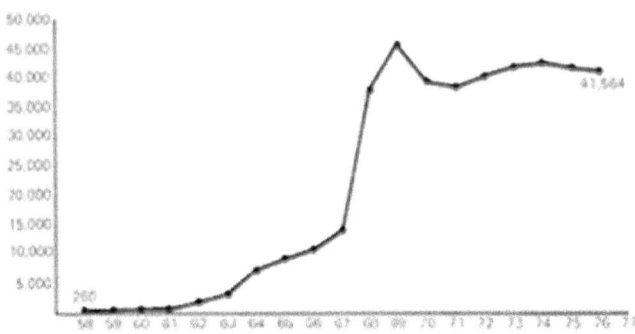

84. CDC Employment History

NK	COMPANY	DP REVENUES $M	DP REVENUES (% of total revenues)	U.S. DP REVENUES (% of total dp revenues)
	International Business Machines	$14,765	81%	50%
	Burroughs	$1,844	87%	59%
	NCR	$1,574	62%	51%
	Control Data	$1,513	66%	66%
	Sperry Rand	$1,472	45%	59%
	Digital Equipment	$1,059	100%	64%
	Honeywell[2]	$1,037	36%	63%
	Memorex	$405	90%	60%
	Hewlett-Packard	$402	30%	54%
	TRW	$350	11%	77%
	Itel	$286	71%	90%
	Data General	$255	100%	68%
	3M	$240	6%	80%
	Automatic Data Processing	$238	97%	92%
	Xerox	$209	4%	100%
	General Electric	$200	1%	80%
	Amdahl	$189	100%	81%
	Computer Sciences	$176	75%	80%
	Storage Technology	$162	100%	92%
	Texas Instruments	$160	8%	90%
	Electronic Data Systems	$157	96%	95%
	Management Assistance	$155	100%	61%
	Mohawk Data Sciences	$146	100%	43%
	Harris	$145	22%	90%
	Data 100	$138	100%	62%

85. Computer Companies 1977

1989 WORLD RANK	1988 WORLD RANK	COMPANY	1989 IS REVENUE	1988 IS REVENUE	IS REV. % CHANGE	1989 TOTAL REVENUE	IS AS % OF TOTAL REVENUE
1	1	IBM	60,805.0	55,002.8	10.5%	62,710.0	97.0%
2	2	Digital	12,936.7	12,284.7	5.3%	12,936.7	100.0%
3	4	NEC	11,480.4	10,475.7	9.6%	23,388.9	49.1%
4	3	Fujitsu	11,378.9	10,999.1	3.5%	18,073.8	63.0%
5	5	Unisys	9,390.0	9,133.0	2.8%	10,097.0	93.0%
6	6	Hitachi	8,719.0	8,247.6	5.7%	49,064.3	17.8%
7	7	Hewlett-Packard	7,800.0	6,300.0	23.8%	11,899.0	65.6%
8	11	Groupe Bull	6,465.4	5,296.7	22.1%	6,465.4	100.0%
9	8	Siemens	6,010.6	5,951.0	1.0%	32,514.9	18.5%
10	9	Olivetti	5,573.3	5,427.9	2.7%	6,583.9	84.7%
11	12	Apple	5,372.3	4,434.1	21.2%	5,372.3	100.0%
12	10	NCR	5,319.0	5,324.0	-0.1%	5,956.0	89.3%
13	13	Toshiba	4,595.1	4,226.6	8.7%	28,896.7	15.9%
14	15	Canon	3,783.3	3,391.6	11.5%	9,791.1	38.6%
15	14	Matsushita	3,663.7	3,441.0	6.5%	40,877.4	9.0%
16	24	Compaq	2,876.1	2,065.6	39.2%	2,876.1	100.0%
17	21	AT&T	2,865.0	2,445.0	17.2%	36,112.0	7.9%
18	19	NV Philips	2,814.8	2,794.6	0.7%	26,981.0	10.4%
19	18	Nixdorf	2,792.6	3,044.9	-8.3%	2,792.6	100.0%
20	20	Xerox	2,790.0	2,650.0	5.3%	17,635.0	15.8%
21	17	Wang	2,697.0	2,918.9	-7.6%	2,697.0	100.0%
22	22	STC	2,643.4	2,425.1	9.0%	4,264.6	62.0%
23	27	EDS	2,477.9	2,007.1	23.5%	5,466.8	45.3%
24	32	NTT	2,254.0	1,694.0	33.1%	2,254.0	100.0%
25	25	Nihon Unisys	2,112.7	2,057.7	2.7%	2112.7	100%
26	28	Amdahl	2,101.0	1,802.0	16.6%	2,101.0	100.0%
27	37	Sun	2,062.5	1,461.6	41.1%	2,062.5	100.0%
28	23	Memorex	2,056.6	2,078.5	-1.1%	2,056.6	100.0%
29	44	Mitsubishi	2,025.7	1,973.0	2.7%	21,032.9	9.6%
30	36	Oki	1,952.0	1,761.0	10.8%	3,858.1	50.6%
31	29	Tandy	1,892.0	1,792.4	5.6%	4,285.7	44.1%
32	31	Alcatel	1,800.3	1,716.0	4.9%	14,086.1	12.8%
33	30	Ricoh	1,799.5	1,727.5	4.2%	5,880.8	30.6%
34	40	Seagate	1,797.0	1,351.0	33.0%	1,797.0	100.0%
35	16	Control Data	1,691.0	2,538.0	-33.4%	2,934.5	57.6%
36	33	ADP	1,689.5	1,617.0	4.5%	1,689.5	100.0%
37	38	Tandem	1.676.8	1,424.7	17.7%	1.676.8	100.0%

86. Computer Companies 1988

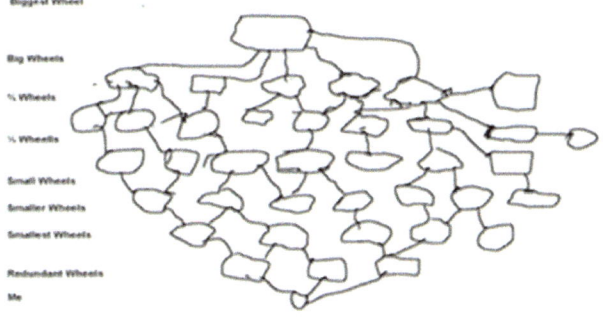

87. Big Computer Companies Organigram

88. Business Disaster

89. The 'Grounding'

90. Is he trying to find CDC?

19. Homage to Seymour Cray.

From July until December 1964 the author had the privilege to be in CDC's Chippewa Falls Lab. He was there to be trained as a CE.

It was not only training. He also was engaged to help in the design of the magnetic tape driver portion of the 6600.

He often had the chance to talk with Seymour Cray. He was very impressed by Cray's personality. The probably most genius of computer designers and already at that time multi-millionaire took his time to discuss with the 'little' shy and very new in the 'real' computer world being Swiss.

Cray avoided publicity, and there are several unusual tales about his life away from work, termed "Rollwagenisms" from then-CEO of Cray Research, John A. Rollwagen.

Seymour enjoyed skiing, windsurfing, tennis, and other sports. Another favorite pastime was digging a tunnel under his home. He attributed the secret of his success to 'visits by elves' while he worked in the tunnel: "While I'm digging in the tunnel, the elves will often come to me with solutions to my problem."

At CDC, Cray's legendary dislike of bureaucracy soon became apparent. One story is when Cray was asked by management to provide detailed one-year and five-year plans for his next machine, he simply wrote, "Five-year goal: Build the fastest computer in the world. One year goal: One-fifth of the above." And another time, when expected to write a multipage detailed status report for the company executives, Cray's two-sentence report read: "Activity is progressing satisfactorily as outlined under the June plan. There have been no significant changes or deviations from the June plan."

Cray married Verene Voll in 1947. They had known each other since childhood. She was the daughter of a Methodist minister, just as was Cray's mother, and Verene worked as a nutritionist. They had three children and divorced around

1978. He later married Geri Harrand and had one son and two daughters.

Cray died on October 5, 1996, two weeks after his automobile was struck on the highway and rolled several times.

91. Seymour Cray, Young

92. Seymour Cray, John Rollwagen

93. The Tunnel Digger

```
ERA 1101
(1950)
   |
ERA 1102
   |
ERA 1103
(1953)
   |
Univac 1103A
(1956)
   |
Univac 1105        CDC 1604
(1958)             (1960)
   |                  |
Univac 1107        CDC 3600
(1962)                |
   |               CDC 6600
Inivac 1106        (1964)
Univac 1108           |
(1966)             CDC 7600
   |               (1969)
Univac 1110   CDC Cyber70
(1970)        (1970)
   |        CDC Cyber 170
            (1973)         Cray 1
          CDC Cyber 205    (1976)
         Mini-supers Cray XMP  Cray 2
         (1985)      (1985)   (1985)
                    Cray YMP
                    (1988)
```

94. Cray's Creations

81

20. Homage to William Norris.

Bill Norris was a very interesting and unusual personality. The author never met him personally. But he heard many rumors surrounding the for a long-time biggest CDC 'wheel'.

Norris was born and raised on a cattle farm in Nebraska, attending a tiny school in Inavale, Nebraska, and operating a ham radio. He attained a degree in electrical engineering from the University of Nebraska in 1932. He spent two years on his family's farm after graduation, helping weather the Great Depression and a significant drought in the Midwest by risking using Russian thistle as cattle feed.

Norris entered the computer business just after World War II. In 1946, he started to build scientific computers. He hired forty of the members of his code-breaking team and set up shop in a glider factory with Northwestern Aeronautics, a major government contractor. ERA was fairly successful, but in the early 1950s, a lengthy series of government probes into Navy funding drained the company and sold it to Remington Rand. They operated within Remington Rand as a separate division for a time, but during the later merger with Sperry Rand, their division was merged with UNIVAC. This resulted in most of ERA's work being dropped. As a result, several employees left and set up Control Data, unanimously selecting Norris as president. Another CDC project that Norris championed was the PLATO system, an online teaching, and instruction system developed at the University of Illinois. The university developed most of the system on a CDC 1604 machine driving graphics terminals of their own design. In 1974, they agreed with CDC to allow CDC to sell PLATO in exchange for free machines on which to run it. PLATO was released in 1975. But it was useless due to its high costs and complex maintenance. In the end, PLATO did see some use as an employee training tool in large companies. But it was never successful in the education market.

In 1967 Norris attended a seminar for CEOs where Whitney Young, head of the National Urban League, spoke about the social and economic injustices in the lives of young black Americans. This speech, along with a summer of violence in Norris's hometown of Minneapolis, greatly disturbed him. He became a champion of moving factories into the inner cities, providing stable incomes and "high-tech" training to thousands of people who would otherwise have little chance of survival.

Norris continually purchased new companies to fold into CDC and eventually returned to the peripheral market in the 1970s. This later move proved particularly wise. It was also during the 1970s that Cray left to form his own company, and quickly drove CDC out of its leadership position in the supercomputer market. This left CDC in second place in the market for a few machines. Soon, large Japanese companies were gobbling up what Cray didn't. CDC tried to regain its footing in the supercomputer market by spinning off ETA Systems, allowing developers to escape an increasingly ossified management structure inside CDC. However, this effort failed, and CDC gave up on the market entirely.

In the 1980s, CDC was left primarily as a hard disk manufacturer, and their series of SCSI drives were particularly successful. But at this point, the rest of the company crashed, and the board pressed Norris to step down. They were particularly harsh in blaming his social programs for their problems, although any connection is difficult, if not impossible, to find. He eventually realized there was little he could do to stop this course of action, and started an effort to place the company under the leadership of two hand-picked replacements. The stockholders didn't agree, and Norris subsequently retired in January 1986.

William Norris died on August 21, 2006, in a nursing home in Bloomington, Minnesota after battling Parkinson's disease. He was survived by his wife Jane Malley Norris, eight children, sons William, George, Daniel, Brian, Roger, and David, and daughters Constance Van Hoven and Mary Keck, 21 grandchildren, and six great-grandchildren. Norris, who retired as chairman and CEO of Control Data in 1986, was often ridiculed as a misguided visionary who bet his company's future on "foo-foo social projects" and was more interested in solving societal ills than generating profits. Fortune magazine once labeled him "a business genius who unfortunately thinks he's a social philosopher," while Inc. magazine called him an "eccentric corporate do-gooder." One analyst called him "the Ralph Nader of the computer industry." Doing well and doing good.

95. PLATO User.

96. PLATO in use

97. William Norris I

98. William Norris II

21. Epilogue.

After many phrases, pictures, and pseudo-philosophic theories, has everything been said about the unique computer 'phenomena?' No, by far not. But the author was, after 1981, personally not involved anymore. Somebody else might continue CDC's history. Which is, since the early 80tis, only a sad one.

After 2004 the author left the IT business. He now only writes about it. The internet euphoria and computer mania then started their furious success on the planet earth. Today, it's the daily bread for almost everybody. And it often also results in daily anger. Computers are portable in every woman's purse and each man's trousers bag. All-time ready. As was said and still is the slogan of the Boy Scouts.

What 1964 required space in the size of a gymnastic hall for data storage and costs millions is today to have on a chip of 50x10x5 millimeters in size. For about ten dollars. The clock rate of the computer is in the gigahertz range. In computer communication, we are from the 50 baud rate in 1955 to the terabits. This is a number with a one at the beginning followed by eleven zeros.

From the point-to-point connections to the global worldwide network. Everyone is everywhere on the globe, always online.

Does everyone want this?

And what is going on over the internet? Mostly spam, garbage, unwanted advertisements, harassment, and pornography are floating around. Thanks to the anonymity of the sender.

Grandpa, you should keep silent! There are not only negatives to say about the internet. There are also a lot of practical benefits possible to get by the net. Whatever one understands by 'reasonable'.

This is like everything on earth: Relative.
Vivacious is, for example, E-mail to nearby or distant friends.
Searching for forgotten facts, unknown terms, and so on.
Thanks to Google and Wikipedia! Without these facilities, this
book could never have been written.

But, here is a long-overdue quote from H.Aemmeril:
 "The computer never becomes human. Humanity gets
increasingly 'computerotic'."

Is the computer a job killer? Of course not. Because they must
be developed, manufactured, sold, packed, and delivered. Let
alone the millions of man-years to create the programs and
applications.

He cannot stop applying quotes. For example: "The past
doesn't let us go, the future worries us, and therefore we
cannot enjoy the present." (Unknown author)

Followed by his awful nightmare: The future could, for
example, be the premature doomsday caused by a 'bug' in an
artificial Intelligent (AT) program for military applications.

But it is reassuring to know that even the latest computer with
a fraction of a nanosecond technology still works with the
same simple principle of 'and' 'or' 'nand' 'nor', 'xor' and 'xnor'
logic. Only the number of individual switching elements in a
processor has risen from thousands to billions. But technology
is today at its borders. The conductor tracks in the microchips
have been reduced to the size of a few atoms. Where is the
limit of bandwidth in telecommunication? Surely somewhere.
And surely there is also for it one day a limit.

Humanity still believes that one day everything will be
explainable. The universe with billions of galaxies, stars,
planets, comets, and meteorites. The human brain, with 80
billion brain cells and millions of kilometers of nerve fibers.
(Scientifically explained in 2019)

Absolute arrogance...

Did you understand? Haben Sie es verstanden? Vous l'avez? Ce l'hai fatta? ¿Entendiste eso? Har du förtaat?

The author's last quote:
 "The more he knows, the more he knows that he knows nothing."

CDC disappeared. And many more. And hundreds of new ones came. Mostly from eastern Asia, It is certain: The future development of IT comes from there. Japan, Taiwan, China, Korea, India, etc. Europe is 'out'. The US soon also.

The author told his sons: "Go east, young men. In the west, there is no news." As said in the title of the famous roman by Eric Maria Remarque.
But: "The future is not ours to tell." Song by Doris Day.

By the way: CDC technical flops were not the only ones in history.

There were many others:
- The tower in Babylon.
- The Gustave Wasa, a Swedish flagship.
- The Zeppelins.
- The Ford model Edsel.
- The Wankel engine.
- The vertical starting airplanes.
- The Concorde.
- etc.

And those are not the last ones. Also, future IT giants will fail. This would give a reason for future authors to write a book.

Not for him anymore.

He has struggled enough through the net, often finding discrepancies in was he read there.

The daily, or better nightly, fights with Microsoft's text processor, the grammatical checking utilities, and the language translation programs are getting very annoying when you are well over 80 years.

The first 15 years with CDC were fantastic years. The lousier part of CDC's life did not touch the author. He 'dived' into a new world. The world of the superminis.
This new chapter in his life, will it be as exciting as the one with CDC? Will it also end up in a book?

Qui vivra verra…

Picture Index.

The Computer Evaluation in Pictures.

99. Abacus

100. Babbage Engine

101. Mechanical Adding Machine

102.Tabulator

103. Electronic Tube Computer

104. Mainframe

105. Supermini Computer

106. Vector Processor

107. Personal Computer

108. Tablet

109. Smartphone

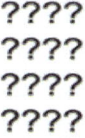

????
????
????
????

110. Futura

Appendix.

The Author's activities with CDC.

November 1963.
For the first time in his life, he encountered the name, Control Data. He was interviewed by a chief engineer from Minneapolis. Was his name Bob Moe?

1964.
Helped to unpack the CDC 1604 for ETH Zurich. First lessons in a hotel (name forgotten) in downtown Minneapolis. Hands-on training peripheral devices in Bloomington, Minnesota: Card reader, Line printer, Magnetic Tape Stations, Disc Drive CDC 6603.Theoretical CD training for the CDC 6600 in Arden Hills, Minnesota. Hands-on Training and active development in Chippewa Falls, Wisconsin, with Seymour Cray, Grec Mansfield, Dave Cahlander, and other great IT designers.

1965,
Installation and maintenance of the CDC 6600 serial Nr. 3 at CERN.

1968.
Hands-on training and active development of the CDC 6400 in Arden Hills.

1969.
EIC for the CDC 6400 at CERN. Technical Support Engineer for Europe: ETH Zürich, Fides Zürich, TH Aachen, Germany.

1970.
Again in Arden Hills. His task now was to write a hardware test and troubleshoot the program for the CDC 6603 Disc. In PPU assembler.

1971.
A new start as a junior programmer for CDC at CERN. Basic

training seminar in Tel Aviv, Israel
Install new COS releases, analyze system crash postmortem
dumps, and implement CERN-specific changes to the COS.

1972.
Sent for training on the COS to Sunnyvale Software
Development Center in Sunnyvale, California.
Then he was an active member of the COS development
team. The first task was to implement the at that time called
'multi-mainframe' feature. It allows more than one mainframe
can access the same disc drives. And what is more important:
The mainframes were able to 'talk' to each other.
What was, as it turned out later, the first step towards
computer networks.

1973-1978.
As a Senior System Analyst working as technical support at
the university of Laramie, Wyoming, Vienna, Austria, and
Bologna, Italy.
Giving seminars at ETH and preparing benchmark Programs
in Ljubljana.

1979-1980.
Assigned to the DIOGENE project at the Hopital Cantonal
Geneve.
Programming systems recovery routines in CPU assembler.
Several thousand lines of code.

1981.
Assigned to the CDC branch office in Lausanne. Undefined
duties.